NATIONAL
GEOGRAPHIC

Grand Canyon
Adventure

Russ Colstan

Contents

The Grand Canyon

Hi! My name is Dan and I'll be your guide. We're going to visit one of the most amazing places in the whole world. We'll see steep cliffs and a beautiful river. We'll also see wildlife and ancient ruins. We're heading to the Grand Canyon.

▼ The beautiful colors of the sunset are reflected on the rocky walls of the canyon.

Our journey starts in the northwest corner of Arizona. Here, we'll find the Grand Canyon. A **canyon** is a deep, narrow valley with steep sides. But that description hardly captures the breathtaking sight we're about to see.

The Grand Canyon isn't just any old hole in the ground. It is 277 miles long and in some places it's more than a mile deep! There are many canyons around the world, but the Grand Canyon is the most famous. It is truly awesome.

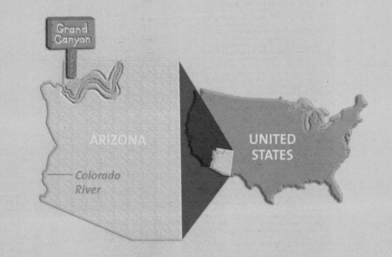

The Grand Canyon is one of the natural wonders of the world. ▶

How the Grand Canyon Was Formed

The Grand Canyon was formed over the last five to six million years by the Colorado River. The river **eroded**, or wore away, the soft rock. Over millions of years, the erosion cut through many layers of rock and formed the Grand Canyon.

▼ **Different rock layers can be clearly seen on the walls of the Canyon.**

The walls of the Grand Canyon hold clues to millions of years of Earth's history. Many layers of rock are found in the steep canyon walls. The deepest layers of rock are almost two billion years old.

Scientists study the canyon walls because this is the only place in the world where rock showing such a large time span is displayed so clearly. By studying the walls, scientists have developed ideas about how Earth was formed.

Canyon History

Native American History

As we explore the Grand Canyon, we see things left behind by people who lived here long ago. Scientists believe that humans have been living here for thousands of years. **Artifacts**, or remains from people who lived long ago, have been found in this area. The artifacts include stone spear points and "split twig" figures. Rock carvings and paintings have also been found.

▼ This rock art at the Grand Canyon shows giant people.

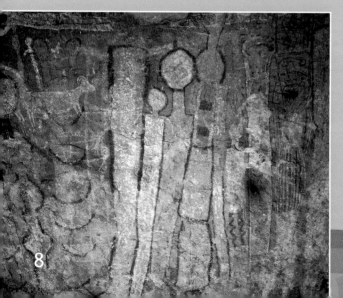

▲ People made this animal figure from twigs thousands of years ago.

▲ This stone house was built by Native Americans hundreds of years ago.

We also see the ruins of stone houses. These are houses Native Americans lived in 800 years ago. Native Americans who now live in the lands around the canyon are related to the people who built the stone houses long ago.

John Wesley Powell

A lot of what we know about the Grand Canyon is due to the work of an explorer named John Wesley Powell. He led a group of nine men on an **expedition** down the Colorado River and through the Grand Canyon in 1869. They were the first white people to travel through the Grand Canyon. Powell took notes about everything he saw.

Powell returned to the Grand Canyon in 1871 to explore further. During both of his expeditions, he came across Native American tribes living in the area. He learned about their **cultures**. Powell also mapped the Colorado River. Later, he worked to share his knowledge with other people.

▼ **John Wesley Powell's group begin their expedition in 1869.**

11

Grand Canyon National Park

Today, when people come to the Grand Canyon, they are visiting a national park. National parks protect areas that have special scenic, historical, cultural, or scientific importance. They are managed by the government.

The Grand Canyon was made into a national park in 1919. The park was created to protect the canyon and the lands around it. About four million people visit Grand Canyon National Park each year.

◀ **Many tourists go to Mather Point on the South Rim. This spot offers one of the best views of the canyon.**

◀ **A ranger shows people around the Grand Canyon.**

Exploring the Grand Canyon

As we explore the Grand Canyon, we'll visit three different **habitats**. We'll visit the South Rim, the North Rim, and the inner canyon. Each habitat has a different **climate**. Different plants and animals live in each habitat as well.

The South Rim

We start exploring the Grand Canyon at the South Rim. Most visitors come to this part of the canyon because of the breathtaking views. The South Rim is covered with forests.

We see rocks with **fossils** in them at the South Rim. The rocks contain fossils of sea creatures that lived 260 million years ago. The fossils show that this area was once covered with water.

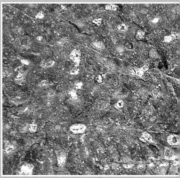

These tiny fossils were living sea ▶ creatures millions of years ago.

▲ From the tree-covered South Rim, visitors can see the Colorado River at the bottom of the canyon.

The North Rim

It is about ten miles straight across the canyon from the South Rim to the North Rim, but it is a 200-mile drive. If you're fit, you can walk from the South Rim to the North Rim. It takes about three days to walk down into the canyon and then up the other side.

▼ **This hole in the rock on the edge of the North Rim is called Angels Window.**

Angels Window

▲ A winter storm begins to clear over the snow-covered North Rim.

The first thing we notice is that it's cooler at the North Rim than the South Rim. It's wetter, too. This is because the North Rim is 1,000 feet higher than the South Rim. It gets a lot of snow in the winter. The Park Service closes the North Rim for about seven months each year.

The Inner Canyon

Now, we follow the North Kaibab Trail that leads to the floor of the canyon. We are heading into the inner canyon. The inner canyon is all the areas below the rims. It includes the walls and the floor of the Grand Canyon. Being in the inner canyon is like being in a different world.

▼ **Hikers look down at the Colorado River from the steep North Kaibab Trail.**

The North Kaibab Trail is really steep. Luckily, we are not afraid of heights! In some areas, the trail is very dry. Desert plants like cactuses grow in these areas. Along the trail we see waterfalls. They gush out from the rocks and fall to the river far below. The air is filled with a fine mist.

▲ There are many beautiful waterfalls in the Grand Canyon.

We reach the floor of the canyon and hike along the side of the river. Many kinds of animals come to this area of the canyon. We see a mule deer at the edge of the water. Mule deer are well suited to the canyon country. They can leap across rough, rocky land easily.

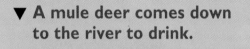

▼ A mule deer comes down to the river to drink.

The Colorado River flows through the whole length of the Grand Canyon. In some places, there are **rapids**. These are parts of the river where water flows quickly over rocks. In other places, the river flows gently between the steep rocky cliffs that form the walls of the canyon.

▼ **The rocky canyon walls rise steeply from the Colorado River.**

Conclusion

Our Grand Canyon adventure has come to an end. I hope you enjoyed it. Now that you've seen the Grand Canyon, you can understand why we need to protect it for everyone to enjoy. The Grand Canyon is a very special hole in the ground!

▼ **The Colorado River winds its way through the Grand Canyon.**

Glossary

artifact something made by people long ago, such as a tool or a painting

canyon a narrow valley with steep sides that was formed by a river

climate the usual weather in an area

culture the way of life shared by a group of people

erode to wear away

expedition a trip made for a special reason such as exploring

fossil hardened remains of a living thing that died millions of years ago

habitat the place where a plant or animal usually lives

rapid a part of a river where the water moves very fast

Index